What funny story did mom tell you that made you happy?

How did you feel when mom was getting buried?

_____

_____

_____

_____

_____

_____

_____

_____

_____

_____

_____

_____

_____

_____

_____

_____

_____

_____

_____

What does mom's voice sound like?

If you could change something about how you said goodbye to mom what would it be?

_____

_____

_____

_____

_____

_____

_____

_____

_____

_____

_____

_____

_____

_____

_____

_____

_____

_____

Have you been feeling differently without mom being around?

How are things been with dad since mom is no longer around?

What do you talk to grandma or grandpa about after mom's death?

_____

_____

_____

_____

_____

_____

_____

_____

_____

_____

_____

_____

_____

_____

_____

_____

_____

_____

What did mom and you like to do during the fall season?

Did you have a nickname for mom?

Do you remember mom's favourite flower?

What did mom say she liked the most about you?

Did mom like any sport and if she did, was she good at it?

What do you talk to dad about after mom's death?

How do you feel about mom not being around anymore?

_____

_____

_____

_____

_____

_____

_____

_____

_____

_____

_____

_____

_____

_____

_____

_____

_____

Write down your favourite memory of mom?

What type of drink did she like the most?

What did mom and you like to do during the summer season?

_____

_____

_____

_____

_____

_____

_____

_____

_____

_____

_____

_____

_____

_____

_____

_____

_____

_____

What did mom and you like doing the most together?

What did mom and you like to do during the winter season?

When mom was ill at the hospital or at home, how did it make you feel?

_____

_____

_____

_____

_____

_____

_____

_____

_____

_____

_____

_____

_____

_____

_____

_____

_____

_____

Do you remember what favourite shoe mom liked to wear?

What did you wish you could have said to mom more often when she was alive?

_____

_____

_____

_____

_____

_____

_____

_____

_____

_____

_____

_____

_____

_____

_____

_____

_____

_____

_____

_____

What music did mom liked to listen to the most?

What did people say they liked the most about mom?

What did mom and you like to do during the spring season?

What would you like mom to know about in the afterlife that you are proud of doing now?

_____

_____

_____

_____

_____

_____

_____

_____

_____

_____

_____

_____

_____

_____

_____

_____

_____

_____

What favourite snack did mom get or made for you?

What was mom's favourite snack to eat?

How have your friends supported you after mom's death?

_____

_____

_____

_____

_____

_____

_____

_____

_____

_____

_____

_____

_____

_____

_____

_____

_____

_____

Are you still doing all the things mom taught you to do?

How are things been with your siblings since mom is no longer around?

_____

_____

_____

_____

_____

_____

_____

_____

_____

_____

_____

_____

_____

_____

_____

_____

_____

_____

_____

What gift did you give to mom that she was really happy to receive?

_____

_____

_____

_____

_____

_____

_____

_____

_____

_____

_____

_____

_____

_____

_____

_____

_____

_____

_____

Do you remember what favourite dress mom liked to wear?

_____

_____

_____

_____

_____

_____

_____

_____

_____

_____

_____

_____

_____

_____

_____

_____

_____

_____

What was the nickname mom gave to you?

What would you like to tell mom that you didn't get a chance to say to her?

_____

_____

_____

_____

_____

_____

_____

_____

_____

_____

_____

_____

_____

_____

_____

_____

_____

_____

_____

What did mom do a lot that made you laugh?

What did you promise mom you will continue to do when she died?

_____

_____

_____

_____

_____

_____

_____

_____

_____

_____

_____

_____

_____

_____

_____

_____

_____

_____

_____

_____

What did mom say you should do when she died?

_____

_____

_____

_____

_____

_____

_____

_____

_____

_____

_____

_____

_____

_____

_____

_____

_____

_____

What did mom say about the afterlife?

Write down mom's favourite food?